Alan Turing's
CODE GAMES
FOR KIDS

ARCTURUS

ARCTURUS

This edition published in 2024 by Arcturus Publishing Limited
26/27 Bickels Yard, 151–153 Bermondsey Street,
London SE1 3HA

Author: Lisa Regan
Illustrator: Gareth Conway
Editors: William Potter and Becca Clunes
Designer: Well Nice Studio
Design Manager: Jessica Holliland
Managing Editor: Joe Harris

ISBN: 978-1-3988-3116-2
CH010469NT
Supplier 29, Date 0823, PI 00004560

Printed in China

What is STEM?

STEM is a world-wide initiative
that aims to cultivate an
interest in Science, Technology,
Engineering, and Mathematics,
in an effort to promote these
disciplines to as wide a variety of
students as possible.

Hello, I'm Alan! Welcome to my brain-boggling, code-cracking, number-crunching puzzle book!

ALL ABOUT ALAN

Alan Turing was born in London in 1912. He was a mathematical genius whose ideas helped develop modern computing.

During World War II, Alan played an important role at Bletchley Park in the UK. He helped design a machine called the "Bombe." The machine was used to decode messages from the German military.

Alan Turing's code-breaking skills helped the Allies shorten the war and saved many lives.

THE TURING TRUST

When you buy this book, you are supporting The Turing Trust. This is a charity, set up by Alan's family, in his memory.

The Turing Trust works with communities globally to give people access to computers.

To help you solve these codes, fill in the grids on page 96. You will also need to create your own grids for some of the more unusual codes.

Class code

Every student has been given a note by their new teacher but it looks like nonsense! Can you figure out what it says?

Top monster! Hello blue badgers class time calls and pow you're welcome skippety hop to cool down the crazy feet new york city year five thousand. Let's boogie beast start stop rewind as it's hot we love you mean cats now to make hay go crazy outside on the beach and like totally have cream cakes some fake fruit fun.

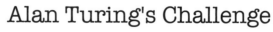

Alan Turing's Challenge

A clue for this would be THREE IS THE MAGIC NUMBER.
Can you write a clue of your own that would help?

Zoo clues

Decode the message on this map of the zoo.
Turn the page for code instructions.

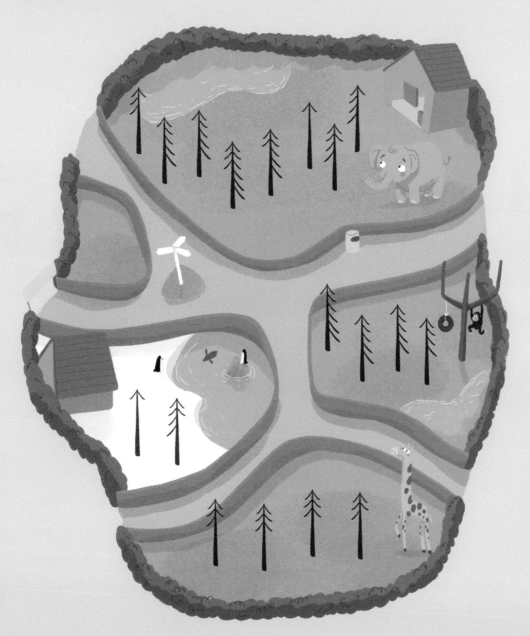

Here's how to read the message on the zoo map.

Each tree represents one letter. The number of branches tells you which letter it is. So the letter H has two branches on each side, and the letter P has three on the left and four on the right.

	Branches on right					
	1	**2**	**3**	**4**	**5**	**6**
1	A	B	C	D	E	F
2	G	H	I	J	K	L
3	M	N	O	P	Q	R
4	S	T	U	V	W	X
5	Y	Z				

Branches on left

Alan Turing's Challenge

Try writing your own name in the tree code to get the hang of it.

Emoji mode

Look below to work out what the emoji message says.

celebrated

meet

emoji

July

any

Monday

tree

look

world

17th

is

behind

day

hour

under

on

Present picker

Lily has picked two presents for her birthday.
Which two items on the list did she choose?

CE

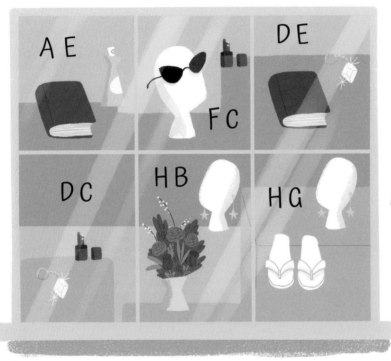

A E

D E

F C

D C

H B

H G

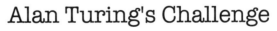

Alan Turing's Challenge

What letter should she say to get flowers
for her grandma?

Flower power

You can use flowers to communicate secret meanings. What flower is named in the code at the bottom of the page?

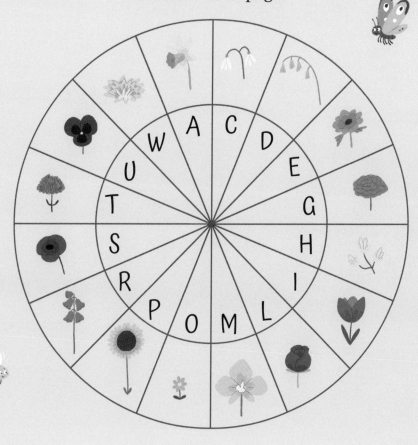

Secret superheroes

What are the secret identities of the three heroes?
Imagine the hands on the clock, with the hour hand pointing to the first two letters of a name, and the minute hand pointing to the second two letters. For example, if a hero was called RAUL, his name would be revealed as half past two, or 2:30.

Names of the three heroes:

A **10:35, 8:30**

B **4:10, 9:00**

C **11:25, 3:05**

Alan Turing's Challenge

What time would you communicate if your hero's name was DINA DAME?

Hide out

You just received this text on your phone. There's an urgent hidden message in the text. Figure it out fast!

MESSAGES

sHall wE stiLl keeP our MEeting at 7Pm? i'lL sEe if thAt reStaurant we likE is open.

tap to reply

Who's haunting?

Which creatures live in this castle? Move each letter one forward in the alphabet to find out. A becomes B, Z becomes A, and so on.

TMHBNQM

BXBKNOR

BDMSZTQ

OGNDMHW

Alan Turing's Challenge

Can you work out the name of the knight who is on his way to the castle?

RHQ OQHYD!

Written in stone

The explorers have found an ancient inscription. With their combined knowledge, they figure out what each message means. Match each ancient word at the bottom with its meaning.

ERAT IN BAKAR HOKO
FEE KEE WAD PA.

MEANS "HE WHO SEEKS THE LIGHT
SHALL FIND IT."

HOKO BAKAR POKO FEE.

MEANS "THE LIGHT SEEKS THE TRUTH."

WAD POKO FEE FEEM
ERAT BAKAR.

MEANS "FIND THE TRUTH
THAT HE SEEKS."

ERAT IN HOKO, NOT POKO.

MEANS "THE LIGHT IS
THE TRUTH."

WAD

HOKO

POKO

BAKAR

Light

Truth

Find

Seeks

Dinner date

A family member is coming to dinner on Friday, but who?
Can you figure it out from the coded message?

vacuum
dinner
soccer
basketball
freeze
battle
beetle
haddock

Alan Turing's Challenge

Can you think of three words to use if the
visitor's name was Bob?

Question time

It's tea break at the juggling school. But there's a question that needs answering first.

Pair the matching balls then rearrange the words to build a question.

The egg-stra difference

Which eight eggs on the opposite page are different to those on this page? Make a note of their letters.

Alan Turing's Challenge

When you have the eight egg letters, use them to spell
the name of an egg-laying animal.

Castle crests

Fill in the missing number for the sequence on each castle tower. Put the four missing numbers together, then use the code to find the coat of arms for the castle's knight.

Tower A: 40, 39, 37, 34, 30, ?

Tower B: 22, 21, 19, 16, 12, ?

Tower C: 36, 35, 33, 30, 26, ?

Tower D: 17, 16, 14, 11, 7, ?

D	E	G	I	K	N	O	R	S	W
6	2	12	4	19	5	7	25	21	5

A

B

C

D

Secret seeds

Mary has planted some secret seeds. She used coded labels so only she knows what's what. Her code moves each letter two forward in the alphabet, so A becomes C, and so on. What has she planted?

EWEWODGTU

TCFKUJGU

DCUKN

QPKQPU

VQOCVQGU

ECTTQVU

QTGICPQ

Find the frog

Poison-arrow frogs have venom in their skin.
Decode the advice to find out which frogs are safe.

FROGS = 1 2 3 4 5

NOT = 8 3 9

SAFE = 5 6 1 7

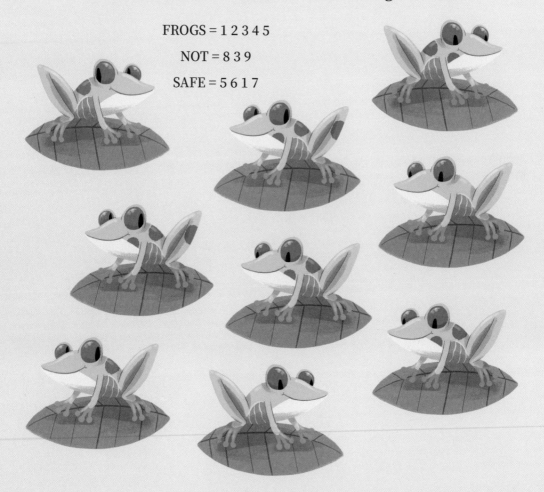

326847 / 1779 / 12345 / 627 / 5617

Money grabbers

Safecrackers have robbed the bank. Someone must have tipped them off about the code. What numbers did they use?

It is one of these four codes:

6227

4138

8262

5854

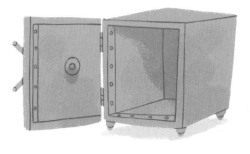

It contains a number lower than 3.

It has a double digit.

Adding two of its digits equals a one of the other digits.

Alan Turing's Challenge

If the clue was: the sum of its digits equals a prime number, which code should they use?

Travel tips

You receive this travel brochure with a strange message on it. On the reverse, it says "SKIP ONE READ ONE." Where should you be going?

THREE ADDS TWO TRY ON MR EX

Alan Turing's Challenge

Which of the sights on the leaflet could you visit where you are going?

Safari secrets

What have Anton and Ally learned on safari?

Clue: read from right to left
as well as left to right.

IRFA
CAIS
EMOH
TOMOR
NAHTE
ATHOUS
MAMDNA
MALSP
SEICE

Potty proverb

Something strange has happened to the vowels in this message. Figure it out, and you will have an important message to cheer you up on a bad day.

MT TMKMS BMTH SMN MND RMMN FMR M FLMWMR TM GRMW.

Password problem

Granny has forgotten her password ... again. Help her access her computer by working out her password from the clues, right.

apple
aardvark
casserole
kisses
slowworm
spooky
curry
teddy

ENTER PASSWORD:

_ _ _ _ _ _ _ _

Alan Turing's Challenge

What do you think the most common alphabetical password, using just one row on a keyboard?

Around the world

Which letters are missing from these capital cities?
Fill in the letters to spell the name of another capital, in
one of the world's largest countries.

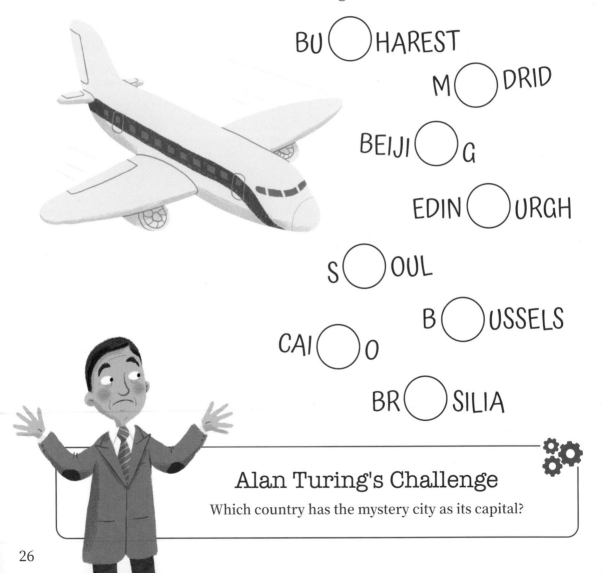

BU◯HAREST

M◯DRID

BEIJI◯G

EDIN◯URGH

S◯OUL

B◯USSELS

CAI◯O

BR◯SILIA

Alan Turing's Challenge

Which country has the mystery city as its capital?

Storm sense

There's a storm brewing. What wise
words does the farmer have for you?

T'NOD TEL EHT NIAR LIOPS RUOY CINCIP.

TI SPLEH EHT SPORC OT WORG.

Spelling test

What is the witch cooking for supper? First, match each label to the correct cauldron using the code. Then use the letters you know to work out what is in the oven.

CRUSTY PASTA

ZEBRA DROOL SOUP

TOADSTOOL TIPS

Alan Turing's Challenge

Tomorrow night, she is making something different; what is it?

✳ ☽ ✳ ◇ ✳ ○ ○ ☐ ✛ ◇ ◇ ✳

Ocean world

Take a look at the map of the marine theme park. Can you uncover a secret message?

✕	◗	☠	〰	☸	→	🍦	⊗
A	G	E	M	O	T	3	4

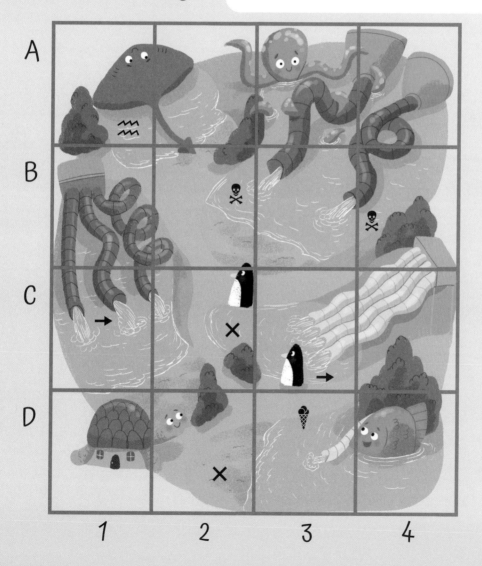

Science star

This box code is simple once you know the rules. Use it to work out the name of a famous scientist and an element that they discovered.

How it works:

Each letter is given a symbol relating to its grid position. The letters in two grids have an added dot.

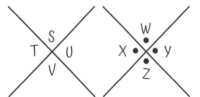

Alan Turing's Challenge

What else did this scientist famously investigate?

Pack a picnic

What's inside this picnic lunch bag?
Use the code letters below to work it out.

E G

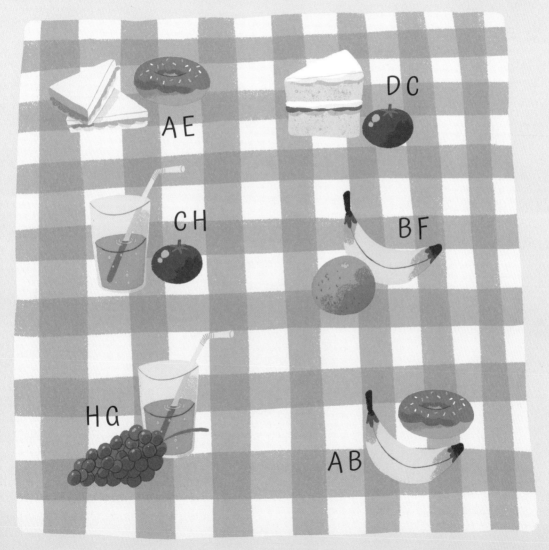

Pirate pals

Join the crew! Your new pirate friends are cagey about their names. Use the clock code to work them out.

Imagine the hands on the clock, with the hour hand pointing to the first letters of a name, and the minute hand pointing to the second letters. For example, if your captain was called WILD WILL, his name would be shown by 4:10, followed by 4:40.

What are the other pirates called?

9:40, 9:05

11:35, 3:50

4:50, 12:25

Alan Turing's Challenge

What time would you write down if you were introducing them to your friend, RYAN MACK?

Round the rainforest

Where are the rainforests? Cross out every other letter, then read around the ring to find out.

The great outdoors

No matter the weather, make the best of a camping trip.
Decode the message at the camping site.

SWIT   NEAN   ITAL
CHOF   DHAV   DOWN
FYOU   ESOM   TIME
RPHO   EDIG

Making waves

How can Alice cross the lake? Convert the binary numbers to decode this message and find out.

Binary is a way to write numbers using only 0 and 1. For the number 1111, from left to right, the digits stand for 8, 4, 2, 1, so 1111=15.

DECODER		
Binary	Number	Letter
10	2	Y
11	3	N
100	4	B
101	5	P
110	6	E
111	7	T
1000	8	D
1001	9	L
1010	10	C
1011	11	F
1100	12	A
1101	13	V
1110	14	O
1111	15	R

101   1100   1000   1000   1001   110

___   ___   ___   ___   ___   ___

100   1110   1100   1111   1000

___   ___   ___   ___   ___

Alan Turing's Challenge

Looking at the pattern of the binary numbers, how would you write 18?

Pet pick-up

The pets are ready to collect from the vet. The labels are all in code. If the mystery animal in box 1 is a gerbil and the animal in box 2 is a snake, what are the others?

Where am I?

Which mountain are Hugo and Lucy climbing? Try moving one letter forward to find out, so A=B, Z=A, and so on.

SGD LZSSDQGNQM

Alan Turing's Challenge

Now move the other direction in the alphabet, so B=A, A= Z, and so on, to find out which country they are in. TXJUAFSMBOE

Morse monsters

Get to grips with Morse code by figuring out the names of these prehistoric creatures.

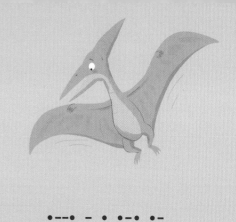

•—• — • •—• •—
—• ——— —• ——— —•

•—• —• •—• • ••• • ———
••• •— ••— — •—• — •••

—•• •—• ——— — •— • ———
••• •— •—• •—• •—• •••

A	•—	J	•———	S	•••
B	—•••	K	—•—	T	—
C	—•—•	L	•—••	U	••—
D	—••	M	——	V	•••—
E	•	N	—•	W	•——
F	••—•	O	———	X	—••—
G	——•	P	•——•	Y	—•——
H	••••	Q	——•—	Z	——••
I	••	R	•—•		

• ••— ——— •—• •—• ——— —•—
• •—• •••• •— •—• • ••— •••

Lucky dip

Luca's parents have wrapped a selection of toys for a lucky dip.
The labels are in code so Luca's friends don't know what
they're getting. What's in each parcel?

Hint: Each letter has moved two
places forward in the alphabet, so
X=Z, Y=A, Z=B, and so on.

RCBBW

PMZMR

BGLMQYSP

RPYGL

EYKC

HMIC
ZMMI

Alan Turing's Challenge

Luca's birthday present is also hidden away.
What will he find when he unwraps QAMMRCP?

Speed star

The name of a record-breaking athlete is hidden here. Who is it? Cross out any number that appears twice. Then use the decoder on page 35 to reveal the answer.

1	8	16	12	3	19	26	21
20	24	2	18	25	22	5	11
4	29	31	17	23	33	10	6
18	13	11	27	1	28	19	8
26	23	15	2	34	14	30	32
5	30	9	32	28	12	33	21
24	3	16	13	25	20	15	10
22	17	29	31	6	7	34	27

Famous first

What famous first did Chuck Yeager achieve in 1947? Follow the instructions to leave the words that make the answer when rearranged.

WALKS

Delete any word containing the letter C.

Get rid of words that end with S or T.

FLIGHT

REACHES   MEETS   MOUNT   HE

                                    CLIMBS

SUMMIT   SOUND

EVEREST   FINDS

        HOT   OF

              FASTER   THE

SPEED   ATLANTIC   FLEW

                    PACIFIC

        VISITS   THAN   CROSS

Alan Turing's Challenge

Move each letter one place back in the alphabet to find out where Chuck Yeager was born: XFTU WJSHJOJB

Online message

Barry and Amanda live next door to each other and communicate with their laundry. What message has Amanda sent to Barry today?

MEET   MORNING   ME   BRING   RAIN   NEAR

FORECAST   PARK   FOR   TREE   TUESDAY   SEVEN

Street food special

What is today's daily deal at Happy Harry's Hot Dog Stand?

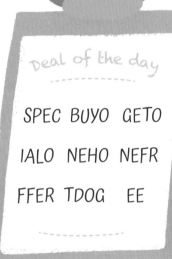

Deal of the day

SPEC BUYO GETO

IALO NEHO NEFR

FFER TDOG   EE

Alan Turing's Challenge

A single hot dog is $2.50. You have $5 but want four hot dogs. With today's deal, do you have enough cash?

◇ ●◇ ◇ ○ ✳ ⊗ ● ⇄   ▲ ◎ ▲ ◎ ◀ ● ◉

Candy store

Madame Bonbon has many sweet treats in store! If the two orange jars contain BUBBLEGUM and COCONUT candies, what is in each of the other jars?

▲ ◎ ○ ✳

◎ ◆ ✳ ◀ ⊗ ✳

▲ ✳ ◆ ✳ ⇄ ✳ ○

◇ ✳ ◀ ✳ ◀ ✳

○ ✳ ⇄ ◎ ◀

○ + ⇄ ✳

Alan Turing's Challenge

What symbols would you write on a jar that contains MELON candies?

Classroom code

Mr. Taft has laid out a message for his class. What does it say?

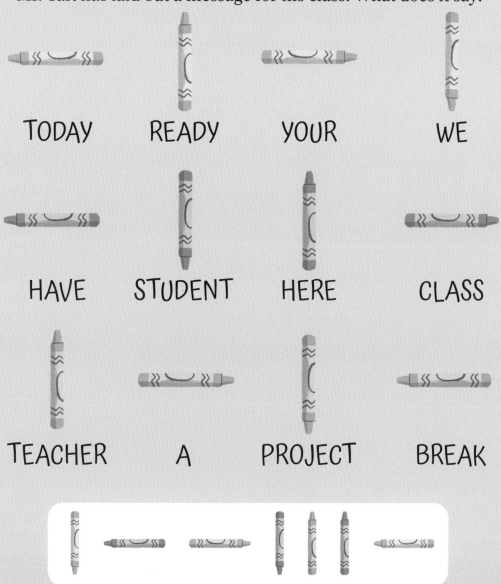

TODAY   READY   YOUR   WE

HAVE   STUDENT   HERE   CLASS

TEACHER   A   PROJECT   BREAK

Map mystery

Your friend passes you a map. Where should you meet her and when? Read the symbols from left to right, starting at the top.

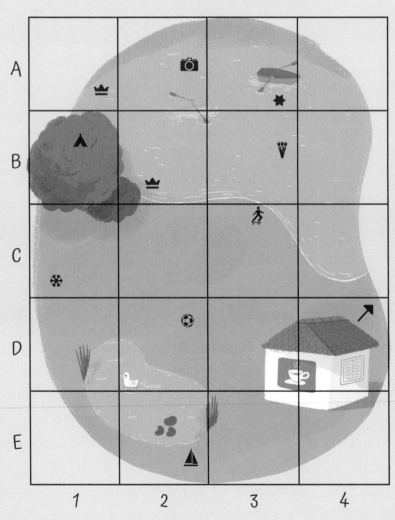

1	🍦	
2	🍦	
3	☀	
4	⚽	
A	❄	
C	👑	
I	★	
M	⛵	
N	⛺	
P	↗	
T	🛹	
U	📷	

A real gem

Jewel thief Covert Carmen wants to extract the precious Stellar Stone from Evil Esme's priceless collection but it is hidden among fakes. Help Carmen crack the code to work out which gem is the real deal.

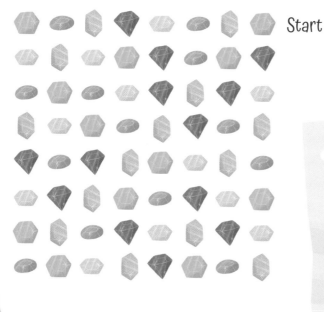

Start

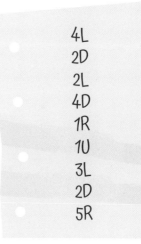

4L
2D
2L
4D
1R
1U
3L
2D
5R

Alan Turing's Challenge

These four gems are alarmed. Can you find them in the grid?

47

Slide backward

Unscramble the coded words by reversing the alphabet, so that A = Z, B = Y and so on.

HRWVDRMWVI

ZHK

NZNYZ

ERKVI

ZWWVI

YLLNHOZMT

ZMZXLMWZ

KBGSLM

XLYIZ

Alan Turing's Challenge

What do all the words have in common? Use the same coding method to encode your answer. They are all...

Sweet sheet music

There's a spy in the orchestra with a stolen dossier.
Decode this sheet of music to find out who it is.
If a black note is a dot and a white note is a dash,
what does it say?

(Hint: Turn to page 38
for help.)

Beach bulletin

What message have this family sent to their friends back home? Work it out using the grid.

	1	2	3	4
a	A	B	C	D
b	E	H	I	N
c	O	R	S	T
d	U	V	W	Y

c1. b4/c4. b2. b1 / a2. b1. a1. a3. b2
d3. b3. c3. b2 / d4. c1. d1 /
d3. b1. c2. b1 / b2. b1. c2. b1

Food budget

Here are today's specials at the Codecracker's Cafe.

€3 24. 20. 26. 21

€9 11. 14. 24. 13. 8. 6. 16. 10. 24

€6 25. 10. 18. 21. 26. 23. 6

€8 23. 14. 24. 20. 25. 25. 20

€7 21. 6. 24. 25. 6

€5 8. 13. 10. 10. 24. 10. 8. 6. 16. 10

If A = 6, B = 7 and so on, work out what's on offer.

Alan Turing's Challenge

What two different items can you buy that total exactly €10?

Tuktuk teaser

Which of these tuktuks should you avoid?
Here's a clue: "Every third one."

TRY LEMUR DO YOU BIKE
NOT GREEN GO GET UP
DOG IN NIGHT LEMON
THE RACE PEOPLE GREEN
MONSTER FIGHT ONE
TWO THREE!

Far, far away

This astronaut has typed in the code for a galaxy destination. What is its name?

a3. b2. a1. a4. b1. b3. b1. b2

	1	2	3	4	5
a	M	A	S	B	T
b	R	O	E	D	I

Alan Turing's Challenge

Which space launch system might one day launch astronauts to other planets?

a2.b1.a5.b3.a1.b5.a3

53

Night nature

If E = B, D = A, and C = Z, work out what animals are hidden in the darkness.

DBH-DBH

FKLPSDQCHH

KBHQD

DDUGYDUN

EHDYHU

PHHUNDW

Alan Turing's Challenge

Some animals are most active at night, while others are most active in the daytime. Use the same code to find out the name for each of these animal types:

QRFWXUQDO GLXUQDO

Chariot champ

Chariot racing was a popular sport in Ancient Rome. Use the code wheel to find out what the victor won.

e tepq fvergl, e 1viexl, erh tvm4i qsri3.

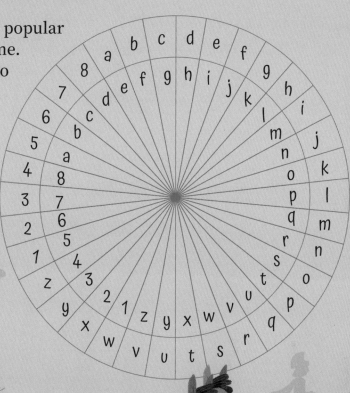

What weather?

What is this man's name and what weather does he like the best?
Work out which letters of the alphabet are missing in the groups to
his left and right to work it out.

Alan Turing's Challenge

Do the same to find his brother's name, and
the weather he prefers:

A B D F G H J K L M N O P Q S T U V W X Y Z

B C D E F G H J K L M O P Q S T U V W X Y Z

Fancy a bite?

Is this a vampire? Use the code
A = 1, B = 2 and so on to see if
he matches the description.

20.8.5.25 / 8.1.22.5 / 18.5.4 / 5.25.5.19 /

1.14.4 / 12.15.14.7 / 23.8.9.20.5 /

8.1.9.18 /. / 19.15.13.5 / 3.1.14 /

20.21.18.14 / 9.14.20.15 /

1 / 23.15.12.6 /. /

Festive message

Find pairs of decorations that match, and use the letters to spell four things you might have at Christmas.

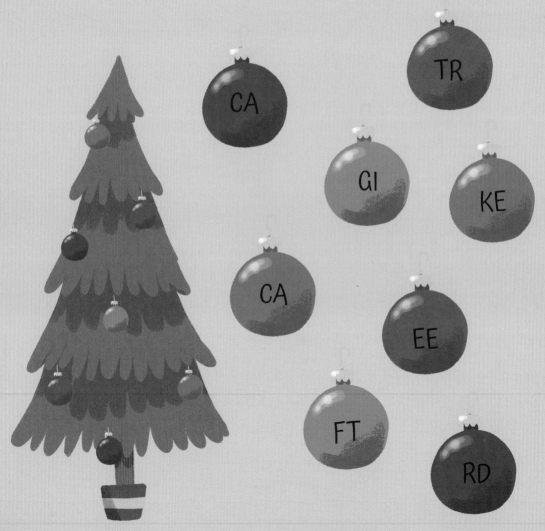

Famous names

Solve the grid puzzle, following the instructions. Place five stars in the empty grid. Each row, column, and outlined shape must have only one star. One has been done for you.

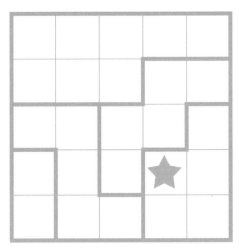

Then match the stars with the letters in the same place in the letter grid. Reading from top to bottom, which famous artist do they spell the name of?

B	X	K	U	P
F	R	I	D	A
Q	H	C	S	G
E	M	Y	L	V
O	T	N	W	J

Alan Turing's Challenge

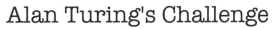

One row in the letter grid spells this artist's first name. Can you find it?

Chilling at the beach

What ice cream does Tilly want today? Use the matching flags to give grid references. Start by matching the red flags to give you the grid reference b2 = C.

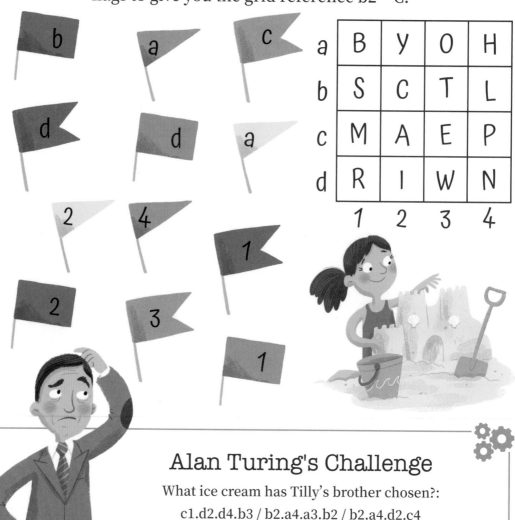

	1	2	3	4
a	B	Y	O	H
b	S	C	T	L
c	M	A	E	P
d	R	I	W	N

Alan Turing's Challenge

What ice cream has Tilly's brother chosen?:
c1.d2.d4.b3 / b2.a4.a3.b2 / b2.a4.d2.c4

Metal work

What is this robot's special skill? Zigzag along the purple and then the pink squares to find out.

Minotaur maze

In Greek myth, the Minotaur was a monster that lived in a maze. Help him find a way across the number maze, using the message. First, encode it into numbers, using A = 1, B = 2, and so on.

THIS IS THE ROUTE YOU SHOULD TAKE

Special delivery

You receive an envelope with a secret message inside. What does it say?

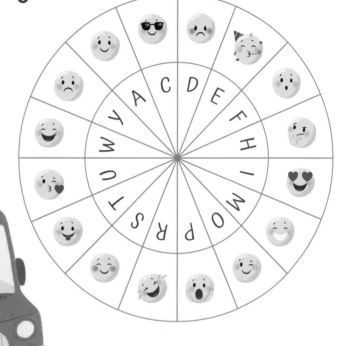

Alan Turing's Challenge

If you want to know where to head, move each of these letters forward two in the alphabet:

AMSLRPWQGBC

High rise

Put these skyscrapers in order from tallest to smallest to spell the name of their location.

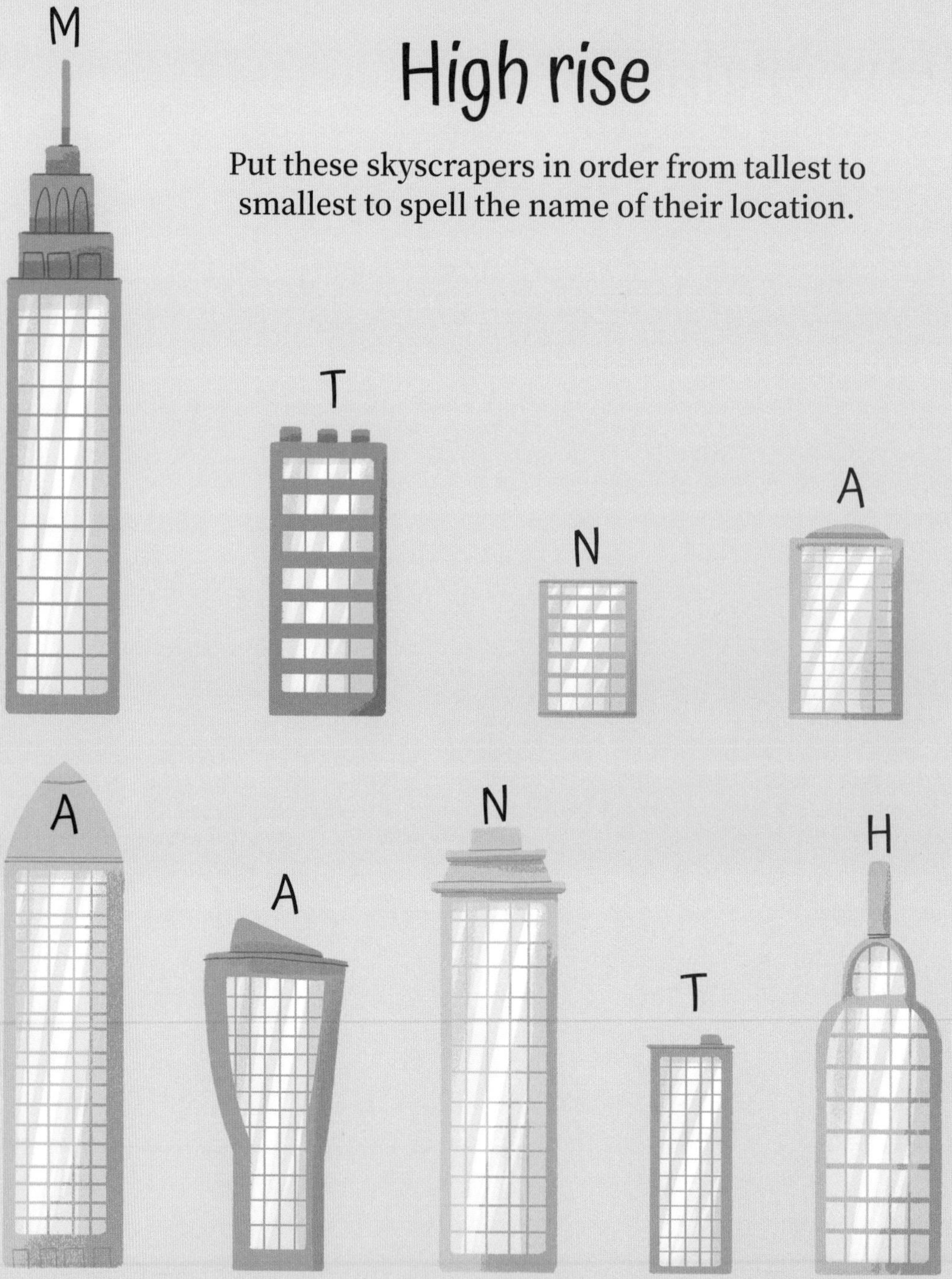

M

T

N

A

A

A

N

T

H

Out in the cold

Spot the snowflakes that don't have six points. Use the letters to spell the name of a polar explorer, reading from left to right, and top to bottom.

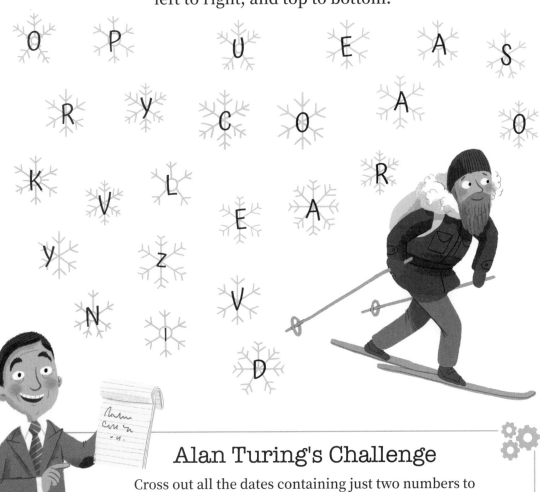

O P U E A S
R Y C O A O
K V L R
E A
Y Z
V
N
I
D

Alan Turing's Challenge

Cross out all the dates containing just two numbers to find the year in which this person reached the North Pole solo.

1881 2002 1919 2020 1994 1991 1818

Twist and turn

The dials on this machine have been moved to the wrong position. Work out the 4-digit code to reset them.

The first and third digits total 7.

The last digit is bigger than any of the others.

The first digit is half of the second digit.

The third digit is an odd number bigger than 1.

The second digit is greater than 5.

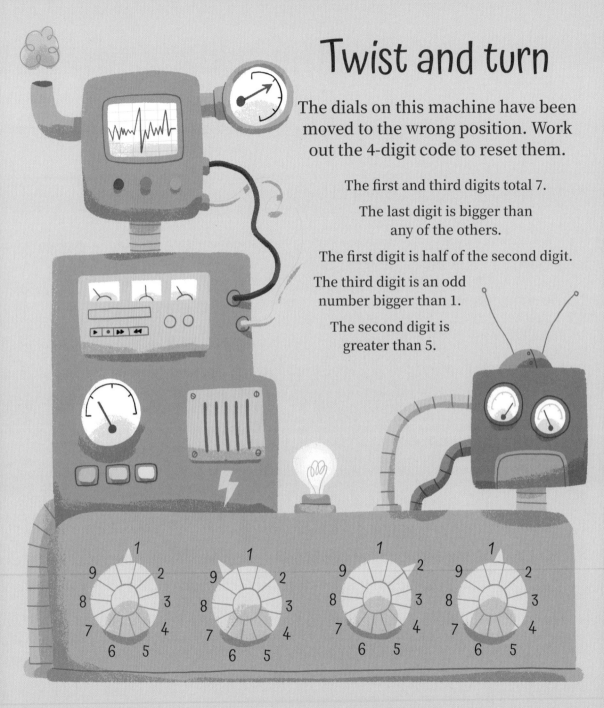

Winged wonder

Use the eggs with odd numbers to spell the name of this flightless bird from New Zealand.

6 - C
5 - K
9 - A
12 - O
8 - C
3 - K
4 - W
7 - P
10 - I
11 - A
2 - T
14 - E
1 - O
16 - L
6 - O

Alan Turing's Challenge

Talking of flightless birds: if a CASSOWARY is XZHHLDZIB and a KING PENGUIN is PRMT KVMTFRM, what kind of bird is a PRDR?

Missing myths

Work out which letters are missing from the alphabet below. Then, rearrange them to find out the name of a mythical creature.

Z   G

J   V

Q   y   K

B

R   S

C

F   L   D

T   M

W   A   U

Alan Turing's Challenge

Reverse the alphabet, so that A = Z, B = Y, and so on, to find the name of a mythical monster who had snakes for hair. NVWFHZ

Off to see the wizard

This merry band of adventurers has a meeting with a mighty wizard.

His name has been concealed within this list. Find the common letter shared by each of the four names on each row to reveal it.

Jose	Jesse	Benjamin	Sanjay
Abdul	Douglas	Juan	Bruce
Albert	Ralph	Logan	Kyle
Gabriel	Elijah	Vincent	Patrick
Austin	Samuel	Joshua	Eugene
Charles	Ashar	Christopher	Sean

Space debuts

Use the code wheel (from the inside ring out)
to find the name of the first woman in space:
ydohqwlqd whuhvknryd

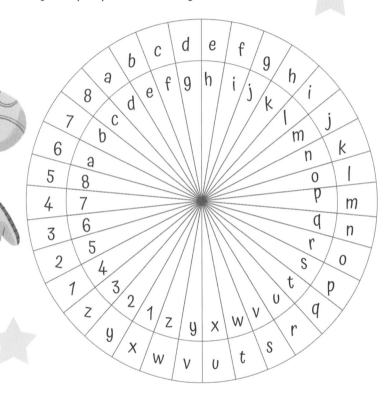

Alan Turing's Challenge

Now use the code wheel to find the name
of the first man in space.
2xul jdjdulq

Frosty fun

Follow the instructions to answer this joke:

What do you call a snowman in the summer?

POPSICLE SCORCH SUNSCREEN

RED WARM SUNNY THE

HOT WON'T

TOO

WANTS WHICH

WEATHER DESERT A

WHITE ROAST

FLAMES

MAN PUDDLE

WINTER WONDER

Cross out words beginning with W.

Get rid of words with three letters.

Lose all the words with S in them.

Once upon a time

Use the grid code to discover two fabulous fairy tales:

	1	2	3	4	5
a	B	W	T	Q	J
b	I	U	F	L	D
c	C	E	K	A	R
d	Y	V	M	H	Z
e	P	G	O	S	N

c5. b2. d3. e1. c2. b4. e4. a3.
b1. b4. a3. e4. c3. b1. e5

a1. c2. c4. b2. a3. d1 / c4. e5. b5 /
a3. d4. c2 / a1. c2. c4. e4. a3

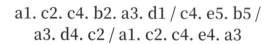

Alan Turing's Challenge

Use the same grid to find the name of a
famous writer of fairy tales:
c1. d4. c4. c5. b4. c2. e4 / e1. c2. c5. c5. c4. b2. b4. a3

Say it with jewels

Work out the messages hidden in each of these bracelets.

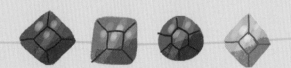

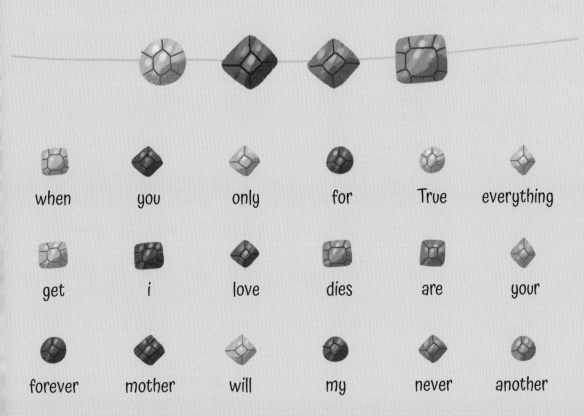

when   you   only   for   True   everything

get   i   love   dies   are   your

forever   mother   will   my   never   another

Seeking shelter

It's pouring with rain but you need a code to get indoors. Work out the three numbers that need to be typed in to the keypad.

| 1 | 2 | 3 | 4 | 5 |
| 6 | 7 | 8 | 9 | # |

752	One number is correct and in the right position
316	No numbers are correct
821	Two numbers are correct but in the wrong position
538	One number is correct but in the wrong position
714	One number is correct but in the wrong position

Motto for life

These emojis have a fun message for you.
Can you work out what it is?

HAPPY   LOOK   WHO   SMILE   TIME   CAN   RUN

MAKES   THOSE   FIND   YOUR   SUNSHINE

BACK   EVERYONE   WAIT   RAINBOW

Alan Turing's Challenge

Try making up your own sentences using just these emojis.

It takes two

These two friends must join forces to discover the plan. They know the first word of the message is "MEET". Can you decode the rest?

HOME
MINE
INFO
FEAR
WIFI
PAPA
INFO

ETHANE
ARMY
ODDITY
EASY
VEST
STOP
URGE

Take your seats

Miss Maybee has put her students' names around the table using a code, moving each letter two back in the alphabet, so A=C, B=D, Z=B, and so on. What are the students' names?

Kgjcq

Kmjjw

Kgqqw

Kmlrw

Kypgm

Kyqml

Alan Turing's Challenge

Two of the students are twins.
Using the same code, work out who they are.
RFCW FYTC BMSZJC JCRRCPQ GL RFCGP LYKCQ

Just for fun

What cheerful message is hidden in the grid? Follow the instructions, starting with the letter A, to find out.

A	C	U	G	L	I	X	D	A	G
G	Y	E	P	S	A	F	S	M	I
R	O	B	Z	V	J	H	W	E	G
I	P	O	C	D	B	N	H	O	G
N	U	L	T	Y	R	K	T	V	L
G	M	O	D	E	F	H	A	G	E
Q	Z	E	R	L	G	H	F	S	A
Q	R	S	H	N	U	I	B	W	L
P	Y	D	O	R	X	G	J	C	U
A	C	H	U	C	K	L	E	T	K

Start

5U 2R 2U 2R / 3D 5R 2D 3L 3U / 3U 2R 2U 4L 1D /

3L 1D 2D 3D / 2R 2R 3U 2R 3U

Alan Turing's Challenge

Can you find three other words linked to laughter, hidden around the grid?

First date

What plans do these code-loving teens have? Read in a spiral starting from top right to find out.

S E V E N R
T Y A M F O
A B E O O L
G D I V L L
N E W O L E
I T A K S R

The top job

Trace a path across the grid stepping only on numbers from the seven times table.

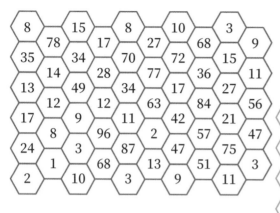

Once you have your path, copy it on to the letter grid. It now spells out the name of a former president of the USA.

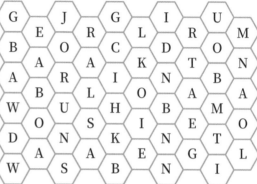

Alan Turing's Challenge

Which face carved into Mount Rushmore is the youngest to become US president? Move each letter forward two to find out. RFCMBMPC PMMQCTCJR

Dressing up

Mamiko is deciding which costume to choose. Cross out all the letters that appear twice and then rearrange those that are left to find the costume she picked.

Surprise gift

What does Mickey want for his birthday? And what is he actually going to get?

rqa1ubrq22

Use the code wheel from the inner ring out to find out.

xuqt6x54ua

An alternative message

What bears live at the
North Pole? Use this simple
pattern to find out: Skip
one, read one.

IVE EAR MY SCHOOL ODD

OWN BEES!

Best book

Can you work out the title of one of the most popular children's books of all time? There's something one book on each shelf has in common with a book on each of the other four shelves ...

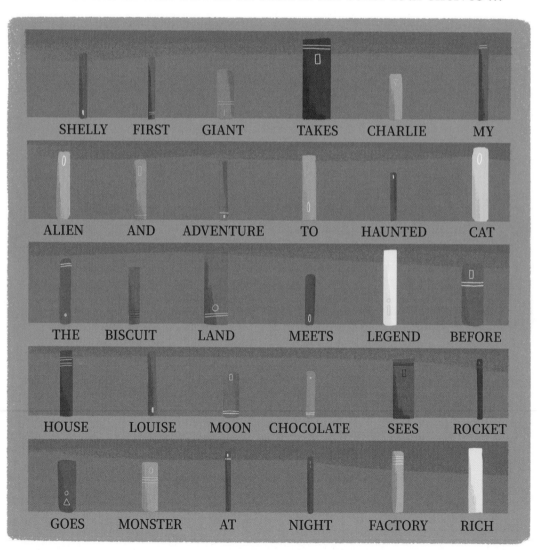

SHELLY	FIRST	GIANT	TAKES	CHARLIE	MY
ALIEN	AND	ADVENTURE	TO	HAUNTED	CAT
THE	BISCUIT	LAND	MEETS	LEGEND	BEFORE
HOUSE	LOUISE	MOON	CHOCOLATE	SEES	ROCKET
GOES	MONSTER	AT	NIGHT	FACTORY	RICH

Clever coder

Somebody has programmed this robot to dance. It carries out its moves in a random order. Can you crack the code and reprogram it to follow your instructions?

1001	1111	1011	The robot moves its left foot, spins around, and nods its head.
0101	1101	1001	The robot raises its left arm, spins around, and claps its hands.
	1111	0101	The robot claps its hands and nods its head.
		0001	The robot raises its right arm.
1011	0001	0011	The robot moves its left foot, raises its right arm, and moves its right foot.

What code would you use to get the robot to clap its hands and move its right foot?

Solutions

Page 4

Hello class and welcome to the new year. Let's start as we mean to go on and have some fun.

(Read every third word.)

Pages 5–6

MEERKATS FEED AT NOON

Page 7

World emoji day is celebrated on July 17th.

Page 8

A = perfume
B = flowers
C = lipstick
D = diamond
E = book
F = sunglasses
G = sandals
H = earrings

CE = lipstick and a book

Alan Turing's Challenge
Answer: B = flowers

Page 9

MARIGOLD

Page 10

A ESME PAUL
B DARA WEST
C NINA DIAZ

Alan Turing's Challenge
Answer: 3:25, 4:35

Page 11

There is a hidden message in the uppercase letters:

HELP ME PLEASE

Page 12

UNICORN, CYCLOPS, CENTAUR, PHOENIX

Alan Turing's Challenge
Answer: SIR PRIZE!

Page 13

Light = HOKO
Truth = POKO
Find = WAD
Seeks = BAKAR

Page 14

Uncle Ted.

(Look at the consecutive double letters in each word!)

Alan Turing's Challenge

Answer: You could have bubble, moon, hobby, or robber, fool, rabbit, or other combinations of words containing those consecutive double letters.

Solutions

Page 15

DOES KATE LIKE MILK?

Pages 16–17

Alan Turing's Challenge
Answer: TORTOISE.

Page 18

40	22	36	17
39	21	35	16
37	19	33	14
34	16	30	11
30	12	26	7
25	7	21	2
R	O	S	E

The castle's knight is D, with the rose as his coat of arms.

Page 19

EWEWODGTU = CUCUMBERS

TCFKUJGU = RADISHES

DCUKN = BASIL

QPKQPU = ONIONS

VQOCVQGU = TOMATOES

ECTTQVU = CARROTS

QTGICPQ = OREGANO

Page 20

ORANGE FEET FROGS ARE SAFE.

Page 21

The code used was 8262.

Alan Turing's Challenge
Answer: 6227 (6 + 2 + 2 + 7 = 17).

Page 22

HEAD TO ROME

Alan Turing's Challenge
Answer: Rome is in Italy, and home to the Colosseum (pictured bottom right).

Solutions

Page 23

AFRICA IS HOME TO MORE THAN A THOUSAND MAMMAL SPECIES.

Page 24

All the vowels have been replaced with the letter M. Once corrected, the message reads:

IT TAKES BOTH SUN AND RAIN FOR A FLOWER TO GROW.

Page 25

Granny's password is made up of one of the consecutive double letters in each word: PASSWORD.

She really needs to change it!

Alan Turing's Challenge

Answer: The most common password is "qwerty."

Page 26

BUCHAREST

MADRID

BEIJING

EDINBURGH

SEOUL

BRUSSELS

CAIRO

BRASILIA

The missing letters spell CANBERRA

Alan Turing's Challenge

Answer: Australia

Page 27

DON'T LET THE RAIN SPOIL YOUR PICNIC. IT HELPS THE CROPS TO GROW.

(Each word has its letters going backward.)

Page 28

1 TOADSTOOL TIPS.

2 CRUSTY PASTA.

3 ZEBRA DROOL SOUP.

Using those letters and symbols, you can work out that she has BAT EYE PIE in the oven! Yum!

Alan Turing's Challenge

Answer: EYEBALL PIZZA! Double yum!

Page 29

MEET AT A3

Page 30

MARIE CURIE

POLONIUM

Alan Turing's Challenge

Answer: RADIOACTIVITY

Solutions

Page 31

A = donut

B = banana

C = tomato

D = cake

E = sandwich

F = orange

G = grapes

H = juice

EG = sandwich and grapes.

Page 32

TALL TARA

MEAN MARY

WIRY WALT

Alan Turing's Challenge

Answer: 10:35, 3:30

Page 33

EVERY CONTINENT EXCEPT ANTARCTICA.

Page 34

SWITCH OFF YOUR PHONE AND HAVE SOME DIGITAL DOWNTIME. (Read each column from top to bottom, then left to right.)

Page 35

0101 = 5

1100 = 12

1000 = 8

1000 = 8

1001 = 9

0110 = 6

0100 = 4

1110 = 14

1100 = 12

1111 = 15

1000 = 8

PADDLEBOARD

Alan Turing's Challenge

Answer: In binary, 18 is written 10010

Page 36

The other labels read:
1. GERBIL, 2. SNAKE,
3. RABBIT, 4. RAT,
5. KITTEN, 6. BIRD.

Page 37

Move one letter forward to get: THE MATTERHORN

Alan Turing's Challenge

Answer: Move one letter backward to get: SWITZERLAND

Page 38

PTERANODON

DROMAEOSAURUS

PLESIOSAURUS

EUOPLOCEPHALUS

Solutions

Page 39

TEDDY

ROBOT

DINOSAUR

TRAIN

GAME

JOKE BOOK

Alan Turing's Challenge

Answer: SCOOTER

Page 40

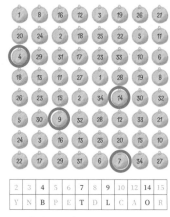

2	3	4	5	6	7	8	9	10	12	14	15
Y	N	B	P	E	T	D	L	C	A	O	R

Bolt (Usain).

Page 41

HE FLEW FASTER THAN THE SPEED OF SOUND.

Alan Turing's Challenge

Answer: WEST VIRGINIA

Page 42

RAIN FORECAST FOR TUESDAY MORNING.

Page 43

SPECIAL OFFER BUY ONE HOT DOG GET ONE FREE

(Read each column from top to bottom, then left to right.)

Alan Turing's Challenge

Answer: Yes – the special offer means you have exactly enough for four hot dogs.

Page 44

COLA

ORANGE

CARAMEL

BANANA

LEMON

LIME

Alan Turing's Challenge

Answer: ⇉ ✳ ○ ◎ ◀

Solutions

Page 45

WE HAVE A STUDENT
TEACHER HERE TODAY.

Page 46

C U IN C2 AT 4PM

See you in C2 at 4PM.

Page 47

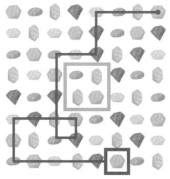

The code means 4L = 4 steps
left, 2D = 2 steps down, etc.

Alan Turing's Challenge

Answer: Shown in green
square.

Page 48

SIDEWINDER

ASP

MAMBA

VIPER

ADDER

BOOMSLANG

ANACONDA

PYTHON

COBRA

Alan Turing's Challenge

Answer: They are all snakes:
HMZPVH

Page 49

The harpist has the file.

Page 50

ON THE BEACH.
WISH YOU WERE HERE.

Page 51

SOUP

FISHCAKES

TEMPURA

RISOTTO

PASTA

CHEESECAKE

Alan Turing's Challenge

Answer: Soup and pasta.

Page 52

DO NOT GET IN THE GREEN
ONE! (Read every third word.)

Solutions

Page 53

The SOMBRERO galaxy. It is about 28 million light years from Earth.

Alan Turing's Challenge

Answer: ARTEMIS

Page 54

AYE-AYE

CHIMPANZEE

HYENA

AARDVARK

BEAVER

MEERKAT

Alan Turing's Challenge

Answer: NOCTURNAL DIURNAL

Page 55

A palm branch, a wreath, and prize money.

Page 56

JAMES, SNOW

Alan Turing's Challenge

Answer: ERIC, RAIN

Page 57

THEY HAVE RED EYES AND LONG WHITE HAIR. SOME CAN TURN INTO A WOLF.

He certainly has red eyes and long white hair. Don't take any chances!

Page 58

CARD,
TREE,
GIFT,
CAKE

Page 59

B	X	K	U	P
F	R	I	D	A
Q	H	C	S	G
E	M	Y	L	V
O	T	N	W	J

KAHLO

Alan Turing's Challenge

Answer: FRIDA

Solutions

Page 60
CHERRY

Alan Turing's Challenge
Answer: MINT CHOC CHIP

Page 61
SEARCH AND RESCUE

Page 62
THIS IS THE ROUTE YOU
SHOULD TAKE =

20, 8, 9, 19   9, 19   20, 8, 5

18, 15, 21, 20, 5   25, 15, 21

19, 8, 15, 21, 12, 4   20, 1, 11, 5

Page 63
FARMHOUSE

Alan Turing's Challenge
Answer: COUNTRYSIDE

Page 64
MANHATTAN

Page 65
(Børge) OUSLAND (Norwegian explorer).

Alan Turing's Challenge
Answer: 1994

Page 66
4839

Page 67

6-C   5-K   9-A

12-O   8-C

4-W   3-K

11-A   2-T   7-P   10-I   14-E

1-O   16-L   6-O

KAKAPO

Alan Turing's Challenge
Answer: KIWI. (Reverse the alphabet so A = Z, B = Y, etc.)

Solutions

Page 68

PHOENIX

Alan Turing's Challenge

Answer: MEDUSA.

Page 69

JULIUS

Page 70

Valentina Tereshkova

Alan Turing's Challenge

Answer: Yuri Gagarin

Page 71

What do you call a snowman in the summer?

A PUDDLE!

Page 72

RUMPELSTILTSKIN,
BEAUTY AND THE BEAST

Alan Turing's Challenge

Answer: CHARLES PERRAULT

Page 73

You are my everything.

True love never dies.

Page 74

482

Page 75

YOUR SMILE MAKES
EVERYONE HAPPY

Page 76

MEET NEAR FOOD AREA,
FIVE PAST FOUR

Page 77

The names are: Miles, Molly,
Missy, Monty, Mario, and
Mason.

Alan Turing's Challenge

Answer: The code reads: THEY
HAVE DOUBLE LETTERS IN
THEIR NAMES. So Molly and
Missy are twins.